In Praise of
Ayeyemi's Works

Taofeek Ayeyemi's collection, *Aubade at Night or Serenade in the Morning*, without fear, calls out police corruption, abuse, and exploitation in Nigeria. These powerful and brave poems weave together nation and body, political and personal, loathing and reverence for a homeland that is "…a clot of spilled blood / and everyone has his fingers / reeking of redness." Taofeek's collection is simply stunning, haunting, needed and beautifully so; each poem leaves you wrecked and in awe. Poem by poem, Ayeyemi builds a bruised and wounded world in which we understand that the unfathomable exists, but that hope will not be crippled as "the power we tuck in our minds will make a walking stick / it will make for the journey an undying light. call it a legacy."

— Tayve Neese
Executive Editor, *Trio House Press* and *Banyan Review*

In *Aubade at Night or Serenade in the Morning*, Taofeek Ayeyemi writes "'there are things that poetry can't cure,'/but" as he goes on to say "silence is dangerous it casts a noise-proof/veil against the voices of the crying & the dying." What Ayeyemi orbits in his stunning collection is a perpetual violence and resilience spinning in an endless cycle "because living, for me, is to die a daily death & be birthed again into mirth." This collection, with the vastness of Ayeyemi's poetic language, explores multitudes—from the corruption of a country, to love's heartbreak, from familial lore to the spirit/ual underpinnings of life in this world. Reading Ayeyemi's words is like spending time with a sacred text.

— Sara Lefsyk
Editor-in-Chief, *Ethel Zine & Micro Press*

AUBADE AT NIGHT
OR
SERENADE IN THE MORNING

FLOWERSONG
PRESS

poems by
taofeek ayeyemi

FLOWERSONG
P R E S S

FlowerSong Press
Copyright © 2021 by taofeek ayeyemi
ISBN: 978-1-953447-80-7
Library of Congress Control Number: 2021942542

Published by FlowerSong Press
in the United States of America.
www.flowersongpress.com

Cover art: "Los días oscuros" 262
by Octavio quintanilla
IG: @writeroctavioquintanilla

Cover Art Design by Priscilla Celina Suarez
Set in Adobe Garamond Pro

AUBADE AT NIGHT OR SERENADE IN THE MORNING

poems by

taofeek ayeyemi

FOREWORD

The postcolonial Nigeria is fraught with manifold problems birthed by bad leadership. This is evident in the works of the previous generations, which include the likes of Wole Soyinka, Niyi Osundare, J.P. Clark, and others. These writers engaged the leaders that reigned after Independence, and many of them witnessed the grim execution of justice and the funeral of hope. They witnessed the imprisonment of the courageous ones who stood just to see that the children of the masses could have access to the resources provided for the children of the rich. Unfortunately, this is 2021, and the rays of hope still dim-- despite the struggles of the predecessors and their engagement of socio political quagmire that destabilized the country.

In the ditigal age, emerging Nigerian poets have carried their cross of revolutionary to social platforms. The influx of literary magazines has created an archive for the publication and the preservation of their works. During the Lekki Toll Gate Shooting, poems were written as responses to failed leadership and zero tolerance of protest and the intentional disregard for human rights by the government. On Facebook, Twitter, Instagram, etc., conversations surrounding the rights of every Nigerian were created. Sadly, nothing has changed, and this reminds us of the placement of ban on Twitter by the Nigerian government.

In this type of system and society, Ayeyemi Taofeek's *Aubade at Night or Serenade In The Morning* finds its root. Reading through the poems, the inevitability of the poet's anger at the leaders and his grievances concerning the quotidian heartbreaking happenings that impede the growth of his homeland is undoubtedly present. He chronicles these sad events with the candor of a poet whose poetic strength and wisdom blaze across the pages of this collection. In each poem, one encounters the experiences of the people living in the poet's homeland, the aches they endure day after day, their longing for hope amidst chaos and turbulence.

Carefully written with each page inviting us to partake in the rites of mourning and grieving the many grim nights of unrest and dread, the poet persona's deployment of language transports us to that state of mind that leaves us pining for comfort and love. In "a land slipping into evanescence," he writes:

 "this land has long been
   shrouded in white sheets
 stained with blood leaking from various
   cuts scribbled on her skin

 by jackals' teeth and hyenas' paws.
  every effort to take her
to the grave dissolves like
  salt slipped into water;

 for scavengers are here
  throwing their talons and beaks
   into her skin, breaking her,
bone by bone." (6)

This haunting excerpt from the collection accentuates the recurring tragedies in the poet's homeland. The images of 'blood', 'cuts', 'jackals', and 'hyenas' depict these sad realities, and we become enmeshed in the gloom that permeates the poem from the beginning to the end. Also, this excerpt brings to the fore what we must know about the persona's homeland, and how to, in our hearts, create empathy and sympathy. In the news, the presence of war stretches to everywhere. Daily, news about Boko-haram insurgency, Fulani herdsmen and the incessant killings of innocent masses grace the front pages of newspapers. The perpetual abduction of school children and the hacking to death of farmers in places like Ìgàngàn also inform the grimness of some of the poems in this collection. Furthering in his exploration of this thematic preoccupation, the persona writes in "finding a straw for a drowning man":

"this is a letter written with ink of blood.

that our past heroes & gone souls

left us with enough to chew:

a sinew covered with flesh.
a roadmap leading to bitter headlines
& breaking news. a muted trumpet & an àgídìgbo with no
string. a fish on the water, belly up.
a flowering tree but fruitless. a bangle
that's also a shackle – & to escape
is to journey into blood. through a flood." (10)

The drought of dreams and the death of a promised land reflect through this excerpt. The poet persona's use of blood as ink captures the terror and horror that dominate his homeland. The daily headlines reek of blood and the faces of the dead continue to appear in our hearts. There is no promise of fecundity, and this is seen in the lines of the poem.

Other poems in this powerful debut collection attest to the poet's findings about his homeland and the urgent need to document and preserve the problems of this country and the people passing through its tortuous path. You, readers, can delve into the collection and it promises to be daring and compelling.

— **Rasaq Malik Gbolahan**
Author, *The Other Names of Grief*

Contents

dedication

to those who fell while fighting
                for this country or for survival

        & to life
                for being a bittersweet teacher

i

counting down in fortitude

10. here at the riverbank i watch as the egret picks another fish –
    it too has come in search of earthworms to pick

9. this is how hope hands me over to my fear
   can we not pick rose flowers without being thorned?

8. every step we take re-echoes the sound of harmattan leaves
   as if to say a temple bell calls for emergency

7. memories: this morning i rehearsed the way a body shrieks
   when tightened in between logs held by chains of slavery

6. slavery is no more, but the chains were melted into the
   bangles and wristwatches we wear today

5. honey and milk abandoned at the swelling of
   black gold, and like the torn walls of the greenhouse,
   hunger spills over our land like a tired rain

4. a man carrying a fatigued hope confined the body of his brother:
   ransomed, the abductor and the abducted smiled to their bankers

3. this is how flowers
   sprout daily on our

2. headlines in red blossoms. red dews.
   red eyes hoping to behold their gone souls.

   & red hearts in fantasy of seeing bodies
   that collected bullets into dust & ashes.

1. i stare into the sky for a true messiah to descend.

for our countrymen have showed us in act and

0. omission that not everybody on the cross are messiahs.

i witness how this land cut its own wrist

last night's gusty wind chased a giant rat
into the grave, its prints are everywhere

in the muddy soil but the holes are
blocked with the victims of the

pelting rain. the trees are now humble –
bowing to every passersby. they say

the tempest was a pathetic fallacy,
expressing the pain of a land dissolving

into itself, beaten by the monkeys
feeding from its crops even when

unripe for harvest. when musa fled
firhaun to the red sea, he parted

the sea and walked away; this land also
parted its own sea but got stuck in between:

in a bermuda triangle, breathing but
bleeding so much that the sea has turned red.

a judge hits his gavel against a culprit,
it sounded like a jackal giving the hyena

a slap on the wrist. & in days, friends
& family beat drums & the streets to

welcome their sons as if returning from a
battle field. but when foreign justice hit,

you see them going fifty thousand feet,
fifty thousand feet below ground level.

a land slipping into evanescence

this land has long been
    shrouded in white sheets
stained with blood leaking from various
     cuts scribbled on her skin

by jackals' teeth and hyenas' paws.
     every effort to take her
  to the grave dissolves like
     salt slipped into water;

      for scavengers are here
throwing their talons and beaks
  into her skin, breaking her,
 bone by bone,

    haunting and hunting everyone
trying to rescue her remains.
    this land is a clot of spilled blood
 and everyone has his fingers

reeking of redness.
    this time yesterday,
 a dying sheep bleated promises
   shaking the pillars

    and poles of this land,
   painted this land as a
  portrait of greenness,
today, the only thing that goes green

is his vigour:
    our spring is no less an autumn
followed by a winter burst.
    today, this sheep opens his mouth

and all we see is a network
of jackal's teeth.
this land is a pond
of grieved fishes,

    a bigger grief is eating us
    and when nothing is left to eat,
we hope it eats up itself
    into the barest nothingness.

what we remember about this land

after rasaq malik gbolahan's what my children remember

the sceneries of explosion
    dismembering the roofs and walls
of our schools and replacing
    the pupils into the hospitals,

of terrified worshipers scampering
    out of churches into the streets,
following the music of bullets
    into the graveyards,

like when armed-to-teeth security men
    chased my lord off the bench into
his chambers and render the hallowed
    courtroom a hollowed guestroom.

we remember the days women
    hid money in their breasts and
shook them through iron-webbed
    windows to their detained husbands,

the smell of tear gas and how
    protesters wiped their faces
with kerosene while others fall
    like fatigued walls on their knees,

face down, on the tightened grip
    of policemen, the sadness of how
this country turns us to wombs
    of aborted futures, so every day we

get pregnant with new tomorrows
       and midwife the birth of uncertainties.
we remember how bodies
       are gathered behind the mosques

bathed, shrouded, arranged
         side by side like logs,
like canned fish, inside a pit
            and earthed.

we remember scars and wounds,
      people who will carry incomplete
bodies for the rest of their life,
      grandparents with no children

with no grandchildren, sitting
        day and night by the temple
waiting for the next explosion
       or the next inept government.

finding a straw for a drowning man

this is a letter written with ink of blood.

that our past heroes & gone souls
left us with enough to chew:

a sinew covered with flesh. a roadmap lea-
ding to bitter headlines & breaking news.
a muted trumpet & an àgídìgbo with no

string. a fish on the water, belly up.
a flowering tree but fruitless. a bangle
that's also a shackle – & to escape
is to journey into blood. through a flood.

or a flood of blood. they say this land
flows of honey & milk. i've been to ikogosi
warm spring. erin ijesha waterfall. but
there is no honey. no milk. the only honey
i know is a drop i got after a hundred stings.

& to get a cup of milk is to hold a bull by its
horn. as if survival is a war of attrition –
where dozens of arrows are kept in the
ribcages of warriors. as if sneezing into
the morning's air is a sign of complete
awakening. a sign of postponement of

tombstone. a sign that our leaf is not
pluckable. as if cultivating & harvest
has the distance of earth and the sky
but then, when life gets us amputated,
gets us limping, gets us crippled;

the power we tuck in our minds will make
a walking stick. it will make for the journey
an undying light; call it a legacy
call it a succour amidst the collision of

an angry man with a hungry another.
call it a reserved plot of sky, acres of hope:
& one day, a green rain will fall from it.

& we shall leave our own offspring with
enough to bite & chew. & they shall write

letters with ink, a blend of milk & honey.

dirge for mother, or for the day she replaced her kimono

1999, my country decided to try a new style

timeline **adedayo agarau**

my country is in a green-walled autopsy room /who killed her? /how? why?

homicide **adedayo agarau**

at the coming of election
     i hold my heart like national pledge

this is how we insert hope inside
     pillowcases and follow its music

into the dreamland;
     how we lip-sing the hymn of

the promise land
     yet all we have done for decades

is sheer dreaming;
     how we queue waiting to unleash

the fire in our thumbs:
     we make this fire to make our food

it turns our foods to live coals,
     our kitchens to ashes,

our future to infinity.
     democracy is not the thorn

that tore the garment
     of our country's butterfly,

this land is peopled
          by leaders whose hands swim in oil

any egret that enters
          exits as a partridge,

is peopled by fanciers of stones
                a palm oil monger meets them

and gets his pot broken
          into shrapnel, becomes bathed in it.

and they say if you trade
              the wares of sands you will

be paid the money of stones.
          democracy is water is music is aubade

is hope calling our part of the world
              a container and the stars a series

of holes drilled on its body
                  for breathe-ing in and out.

is a kimono adorned
              in fruitful elegance

in loyal foppishness
              to bodies reeking of royalty,

nobility or no-one-ness
              inherited from mother's pillaged peels.

this body is a country and
          my tribal mark is not the only evidence

of my nigerianness,
          the way fire eats us up from the inside,

the way we become decaying
        sacrifices pulling down scavengers,

& the scars left on mother's body
        after being dragged through six

decades of puddle.
            her body still carries the mud

of independence malady
                wet and thick,

but her heartbeats
are melodies of pre-independence.

the bridge of salt

no matter how remote the locality
election materials get there steady
but infrastructural development becomes
a snail crawling on a bridge of salt.
yet, electorates are found multiplying their
fingerprints on the body of ballot papers;
they are found flashing cutlasses
and election becomes a carnival of bullets.

aubade

my voice tickles the dead in the grave. their headstones

shift & slip over the shadows of the tombs, soiling their

aesthetic epitaphs in the mud of july rain.

the crickets' cries add bass to my daggered voice

like the happenstance of fruits falling into the body of water.

from the next-door neighbour's, a more energetic voice

rings out like a goat struggling to cry its last

before the tongue of knife touches its throat.

& amidst these voices, the plight of father's rosary is heard:

the enforcement of its clamour however unsure.

on this balcony that i write this poem, i've asked

where this national curse finds its way to us:

maybe from the tears of the larvae we

didn't allow to grow wings and colours;

maybe the pain of the grasshoppers we picked

on the field and shoved in our pockets to choke; so much

that our sea of rituals could not wash away our hard luck.

& while some takes life fast and furious,

some accepts it slow and steady, but some finds fate

in the roundness of noose or the content of a "sniper bottle."

see how corruption & ineptitude chisel a land into a sad museum?

& since we have no pass to enter another land,

maybe we should meet peace at the border of the world beyond;

& only a dying voice tickles the dead.

breaking news no longer break us

*"***breaking news:** #bokoharam - the nigerian army has sadly lost three gallant soldiers in the latest boko haram terrorists killing that also left eight other soldiers injured, according to colonel sagir musa, acting director army public relations."*

nigerian eye, september 01, 2019

i reread the headline
as if to say it's a fiction,
not because it's impossible. But
because breaking news no longer break us,
because we've been broken again & again
until there's nothing more to break.
because the news came when we were singing silence
to dull the pain of our yester griefs
waiting for the moon to spill its light on our bodies –
for their shadows to pour into the earth's bowel.
how we wish we could rearrange our fate
under the lime tree & retrace our steps into a better land.
or replant the root of this land on another continent,
maybe a rain of sanity will fall on it & wash away
the tumults on its surface & aerate its orifice with
a song of hope & sprout the body of our gone men
who slipped into the bowel of baga, chibok, jos...

quod valuerit caedem

i look up again at the clouds of smoke
climbing up the sky: to dent the stars
of their glee and melt them into subjects
of mass burial, where zamfara is pronounced

from behind. i hear again the sound of
bullets battling one another and
breaking one another's body
into dust & ashes

our forces are now sticks of fire forced into water
and condolences have become overdosed
cover story in the eyes of victims mourning
other victims that went with the smoke

mourning has become the morning sun
where funeral litanies are chanted
& our homes have gone blank & black;
mini mortuaries and cemeteries

i remember a poem that ate me up last night
"there are things that poetry can't cure,"
but silence is dangerous; it casts a noise-proof
veil against the voices of the crying & the dying

fireplace

a train snakes into a tunnel,
i watch as its tail vanishes
into the hazy embrace.
this is how man withers
when his freedom is dragged
from his grip.

. . .

once, i walked into a
maximum prison to see
if i'll find bodies melting
to the heat of the gaol.
an awaiting trial sits
breathing in comfort and
breathing out contentment,
like a snail settling in its shell.

and my eyes query the
sanctity of our prisons,
they no longer correct;
even as they carry red eyes
like a scorching sun,
they only add to the heat
melting down the society;
even though they build walls
against the bodies of inmates,
theyre no longer an end to vices
but the end of the beginning,
a retreat for the robin hoods,
a workshop for upcoming threats.

. . .

only but a few
unleashed the sea of their eyes,
holding the prison wall
as if to bring it down

because;

it was the police who
brought them there when
their palms opened to nothing;

 it was the police who
tied stones around the
complaints of the complainant
so it may sink them
into the bottom of prison.

. . .

a boy stretched his hands
as if to touch my heart,
he said:
i didn't write the confession.
i was touched,
and everything inside me
was activated against me.

the world our tears ask for

i remember how my
neighbour's face was pressed
against the hot stone of

oppression, how his mouth
became filled with sand of
depression, in the hand
of those employed
to protect & secure us.

he shouted, "i think we are
a part of this world."
but his voice faded away
like the tweets of a fleeting bird.

another police lifted him & put
his hand around his shoulder, but
a golden noose does no good:

it is as hell as a black one
like a prison uniform
sewn in satin and lace:
for the friendly police was
only smiling at his pocket.

let's read the following from right to left
maybe someday, we'll get it right
& become an icon of a pristine world:

world a
walk to able are we where
gum chew and

world a
corridor our at sit we where
coffee peaceful sip and

whisky with celebrate or
network carrying without
minds our in fears of

our colouring where world a &
turtleneck black a in dressed & hair
criminals us make doesn't

[i want this poem to fight like a leopard]

for this poem has grown new nails /
the sharpness of razor / it crumbles at
my feet / i lift it into things they say are
 mightier than swords / for what my eyes
have seen / & what my ears have heard /
in this land have made my eyes a channel
of a spring / & a waterfall

//
they said the eye of mercy is blind /
only the cruel one remains / someone
said it's the cruel one eye that milked dry
the light in the other / i don't know how to
explain this cruelty of a thing / how a cop
would leave the culprits / & dump the innocents
into the harbinger of pain / this poem is the
chronicle / [a tablet] of innocent feet / that
have tread the darksome paths of life

//
& i want this poem to run into the villains'
bodies / like a rain of javelin / &
if my words pierce you sharper than a
javelin / say darts / say arrows / say dagger /
then go home & heal its wound / or
carry its ulcer to the future /
if it refuses to heal into a scar

//
yes! let's live this life with blood in our
eyes / as if we've come here by chance /
as if grave is a cave with valuable

artifacts / or an amusement pack
to visit after years of nothingness

//
then one day // god forbid we
mourn our existence // because
we've not lived enough to become dead

portrait of me as a patriot

if you see me ascending the cross, it's never to put
down a messiah, but to dust the face of a well
founded country, showing countrymen this land is only
but gold in the hands of potters. i like to describe
this land as a potpourri of honey and milk, a
landscape of greeneries taking colours and shapes.
let the sun burn me, let the rain drench me;
if you see me fleeting down the cross with red eyes,
i'm not surrendering, i'm only a ram moving back
into strength, for the love of motherland.

i like to think of this land as a potpourri
of honey & milk

if you see me picking up swords & arrows of words,
leaving behind shields & iron vests; the war is for patriotism.

what is that if not a tree root fed with the blood of martyrs,
for the world is a weak plant surviving on the breast milk

left by men taken away. by this i mean we never succumb
to defeat, for like the rain to earth, we're committed to the feat.

baga falls. chibok falls. jos plateaus helplessly with tears
clouding her sight. & our men fall with them.

like independence, i want to change my steps & walk into the
 next level; i want to see red & see the colour & symbol of love;

i want to see black & touch my skin where it sweats out
honey & milk. & this is not a sheer brawn nor an adventure

into emotional sophistry, it is an echo shaking the walls,
polls and pillars of the cabals: for this land is not as ugly

as the rag in which it's wrapped. i like to think of this land
as a potpourri of honey & milk, a landscape of wellness

soaked in colours & shapes. i like to think leaving this country
is like walking out of a pond into a creek, that the value of

our naira can buy a dynasty. even when the number 1
folds the law in his fist & choke it into comma,

i still like to think of this land as a courtroom where

the law wears its full regalia.

they say the number 2's visit means a thing and another:
i. he has come for dust to dust & ashes to ashes
ii. he has come to give 10,000 alms into cupped palms.

yet i don't want his kind of visit, but i still like to think of this land
as a good news. a mail parcel holding a perfumed
contributor's copy of a tasty fiction coming true.

a list of broken things

10. our tongues no longer call things sweet
    until alien tongues call them honey, today we open
    our mouths and our tongues set our progenitors on fire.

9. the veil over our societal eyes stinks of a decade
    ghost, we put our hands in our garments
    of coyness and turn them to rags;

8. our eyes are glasses of nudity the sun no longer
    burns them, modesty is a hands-me-down
    only the silly wears

7. we look ourselves in the mirror and see a thing forgotten
    in the frying pan, a body that's a poem calling for
    urgent revision

6. my sister asked me last night, how do we turn brown
    a burnt plantain? i told her even the white skins bleed red.

5. freedom is defined as a way of carrying yourself
    into the mouth of jackals and become a
    piecemeal on people's tongues,

4. by the people and for the people whose boils and pimples
    pinch them deeper than the australian fire
    eating up the future of some human,

3. than the uighurs people of china, than the rohingya people
    who have become a marco polo on the asphalt
    of pain and fear.

2. my heart is also broken, it has been a hard disk

for a period of aeon now
    backing up grief and trauma. now it can no longer hold things;
    [i'm afraid] even sweet things leak through it.

1. if this line is overstretched, it will also
    break

0. the only thing that refuses to break is this country
    but every morning, i see the footprints of compatriots
    leading to the embassy, for coordinated and documented prison
    break.

leaf by leaf, unroofing our wormwood

when a child is born and bred in a land, we say
his head hits the soil of the place, like a peg,

like a nail, like a seed exhumed from a soil
and replanted in another part thereof,

he didn't walk in there a stranger, a migrating bird,
he is a tree, an iroko, he grew. and because a boy

is born with his legs coming out first doesn't
mean he walks in, he only sprouts in wonder

from the heart of the land, he has his root
spread in the soil like cancer, like willows.

today, i like to tell about this land as a palm tree,
i offer a calabash to your body, pour; pour the

wine of your methuselah, pour the water of your
warm spring, pour the milk of your paunchy

orifices. pour; tie the calabash with a rainbow
& offer yourself to the calabash; pour ceaselessly

for me, for us; for the last night's migrating
birds that tweeted across the full moon were

your scions this land is becoming empty of
vigour & vibes, of hassan & hussein, of taiwo & kehinde,

of peter & paul. this land is becoming populated
with matchets breaking the stones that

sharpened them. but when our makkah refuses
to grow sweeties and fruities, shall we not become
muhammad and take our seeds to medina?

once, a virus irrupted into our land

its name crashed on our leaders'
tongues and broke into versions:
covic 1-9, coronavices, covad;
this is how blind men are made

to lead a community of eyed men
to their promised land.
it came at a time our land was
fatigued and unready for competitions,

much less for war, for pandemic,
for bushfire, for anything that
sucks the strength of a nation,
for this land was already

an aftermath of war.
elsewhere, a country filled
her citizens' pockets with relief,
here, we were turned upside down

and our mouths filled with grief.
a period our leaders fly to london,
to germany, to india like birds
leaving us to ruinous infrastructures.

covid-19 came, banished them
to the beds they left for us at yaba,
gwagwalada, ejigbo, onikolobo;

flagellated them over the duty
to build hospitals, schools, libraries,

and laboratories; and they felt
the augury of posterity, of nemesis.

34

the thing about this country

is that this country is a weak giant/
last night i still heard her sobs/
over the alien dwarfs that entered
through sambisa

this country is an unworthy eagle
that cannot lift a chick/
a lazy lion whose pur cannot lash out
the soul of its prey/ it cannot

unclad its spirit by tearing its body
apart/ it cannot cause wound on
the body of a palm tree/
for wine to flow//

run/ this country is a running horse/
it runs faster/ only in the book
its land no longer reeks of milk & honey/
its rivers have fishes/ that are no longer edible

the thing about this country is that:
its honey/ milk/ & river flew into wastrel /
its fishes swim into extinction
& this country becomes a remnant of treasure

embers

i imagine my body as bashō's old pond:
a frog jumps into it and another leaps out,

can you hear their sounds – the water's,
the frog's? it is sound falling into sounds:

but the mixed music of the ripples and
splashes echoes a voice of darkness

that frightens the dark. as if there's a fire
that will eclipse this pond of pleasure.

as if the legs of my bed will begin to
sprout into an iroko tree. as if a farm of

inferno will grow over my brittle shelter.
by this i mean i carry water (hope) and

fire (fear) together in a cup (my heart):
but this water cannot quench the fire,

it only waves at the sky to let loose itself.
and this body is an album of events

some with teeth contesting glee with the
stars, and some beating one's teeth into

the jaw of a crocodile. and this is how
i poured silence into the mouth of fire:

i.
i chase my worries into the house

it goes to hide in a stack of books and

die in between two pages: this is how i
blow lifeless wings in the air and watch

as it spiders across pillars & poles, and
butterflies between the past & the present:

this ember burns markets, it tars the road
with the blood of travellers, it carries gun

on the highway to harvest fruits & crops
it never planted. call it sept-ember.

ii.
there are things that happen and life
makes you pick a bathrobe in the stead

of a nightgown: i. hunger ii. anger
iii. danger iv. police v. all of the above

vi. others (please specify). and there
are things that stand in the way of fear

looking like light and fire; illuminating,
yet burning, yet giving soothing warmth.

call them lanterns. call them shadows
dancing on the wall. call them octo-ber.

iii.
i pick my teeth and ashes fall off:
it is last night's anger still burning

and my tongue germinates with it.
the wind from my sibling's paper kite

runs through my mouth and blew away
my fear of leaving home. for this ember

diverts the roadmap of travellers to
never return again. or to return in lieu

of ransoms. or to be returned in a body
bag by the roadside. this is nov-ember

iv.
this ember is a bee. it carries words like
pollination, stings & honey in its throat. it

buzzes around carrying ribbons on its tail.
it walks us to the door of santa while we

await the vendor to come with a new
calendar. mother with her phone buried

to her ears. father by the window watching
neighbour's kids burning their parents'

funds in the sound of bangers. in sha allah
this ember shall be named dec-ember.

taxonomy of grief

to take a sick man to a consultant vulture   or a cockroach to the
gathering of cocks   is like keeping a fried fish with a cat is like
shooting a paper kite in the air   without thread   is like throwing a
bullet with bare hand it will spill into the abyss of nothingness   to
tell a sermon of forbearance   to a man flailing in between the jaw of
grief   when you've not bitten your own wormwood of life   or a
girl whose body pour the blood of pleasure amidst excruciating pain
or boy who keeps flying at a fruitful tree fruitlessly   or a chibok
mother who is reminded daily of her gone girls whenever the muezzin
calls   or a dapchi mother whose only bride-to-become daughter is
brought home like a roasted catfish   is to touch grief with a pinch of salt
or lure it to bed & suspend its gloom   & when they wake   everything
rises again and begin to take the shape of wormwood   but until you
show the part of you   where you were broken and are stitched back
to whole   you'd only be knocking the part of their hearts where there
are no doors   &/but/whereas we've all carried plagues in our hearts on
this crestfallen land   writing poems in this land is enough testimony

how this land breeds us into terrorists

i rustle the pages of today's daily,
for a moment,
my heartbeat skips as my heart
rumbles and rattles.

in my country, when we are about
to commit a new civil blunder,
we give it a name, as in a gate
through which hundreds of terrorists
are released while the soldiers that
fought them remained in prisons for mutiny.

this country is a euphemism for joke;
we play too much, so much that
our leaders tie our lives around
a paper kite and shoot it into
a scavenger-dominated sky.

this morning, a boy met on the street
the man that pressed the bomb that
turned his parents and siblings to ashes
while he watched from a treetop.

this is how our fear laughed at us
sipping tea with the crem de la crem

this is how our leaders fetch rain and
water the giant wormwood of our life

this is how our roof is set on fire and we
are asked to sleep heads on hands

last night, a boy watched the terrorists
in the airport heading abroad;
a compensation for making my country
a hotspot.
this morning, i asked him
what he wants to become in the future;
a repentant boko haram,
he unthinkingly said.

how i tame fire into light

on days the debris from syria, sudan,

yemen are lodged in my mind as if my

heart is the place to deposit grief;

on days my healthy cv vacates my draft

and resumes inbox with a pale visage;

on days the tears of wandering rohingyas

flood my thought as ashes begging

for thickness in the touch of liquids;

on days my cooker couldn't heat my

pot of rice for lack of ingredients;

on days the kaboom in zamfara breaks my

hope of "peace & unity" into dark shreds;

on days i wish to make my parents

smile to their bankers but couldn't;

on days i despise events for all i have is

a box of hand-me-down and faded attires;

on days i wish i'm not from this country

on days like this, i look life in the eyes & say:

you can soil me, i'll live notwithstanding.

you can earth me. i'll sprout a woke seed.

because living, for me, is to die a daily death.

& be birthed again into mirth;

on days like this, i write myself a

14-page double-spaced letter,

typed in monotype corsiva, capitalized

& bolded in 72 sized font reading:

today, I chose joy.

43

amen, and everything we say after prayer

amen to the salty ocean of grief gushing down
the sky of our pain. to the promised

tomorrow that came with thrones of thorns.
the pain of blistered, calloused & dusty feet

returning from nowhere. amen to the noodles
eaten raw in the absence of stove,

kerosene. the pain of nights when boys dance
to the hymns of mosquitoes, burning

their pocket-money in the flames of candles.
amen to the worries we muttered sitting on

the edge of faith while we find fate counsel-
ing us of uncertainty. amen to the food we

finish before placing it on the table. to the
longing of waking up tomorrow as a

foreigner somewhere farther from this land.
for this land is now a coffin carrying living

dead. amen to the prayer that i spring off
my offsprings in a land other than this land.

and amen to every prayer i remember after
saying this prayer. so help me god. amen!

once upon a future

to journey back into time is to dig into my root finding:
the iroko tree where its bottom rests;
the whistles that called for moonlight tales
under the agbalumo trees in my father's house
(we've exchanged them today for chlorofluorocarbons);
the gong that called for the king's message;
the mortar and pestle that pounded grannie's yam
and the clay pot that touched her egusi soup where it sweetens;
the footprints of my forefathers when fleeing to the olumo rock;
the smell of blue ink in the letter to my first crush:
days when maturity is to have a hankie almost falling off your back
pocket,
and running a needle through the skin of your palm is courage.

today, civilization comes in the robe of science
and cap of technology: it changes our narratives,
melts itself into an iron door, shuts us away
from the past and banishes us to the present –
a chrysalis pregnant with the future's rainbow.
they say when we add the past to the present,
the future is no longer far from sight; i squint,
i see the future emitting an iridescent green light
in a half smile: call it an insight, call it a foresight,
call it a crab reversing at the brink of a deep bight:
for the world has evolved beyond where we are today,
but if we run fast enough, we will catch up with the future.

ii

objects in the mirror are closer than they appear

and if you want to make the future smile,
call it tomorrow, call it alarm clock
waiting for the next minute.
a boy sees a mango sprout and begins to

dance, he isn't rejoicing over the nodes,
his joy is over the mangoes that will come
on the arrival of rain, it's over the juice.
every morning i clear the compound,

leaf by leaf; i look at the leaves yet to fall
asking them which will fall by tomorrow:
let me pluck you once and for all.
minutes ago, i look into the mirror,

dozens of cars rushing up behind;
the caption on the mirror struck me
as if to tell me to speed up, as if
to tell me to run for my life.

i stepped on the brake by this i told life
i'm not in competition with anybody:
this is how complacency turns our tongues
into faith binding the candles of fate.

in the heart of famine, i sleep on the mat
smiling at the sky. the moon asks
who gave me pounded yam and
promised me a soup fit for kings;

tomorrow! said i.
i look into the mirror

for the umpteenth time, i saw tombstones.
i reread the caption on the mirror.

how fear beats us into bravery

first, we are chicks running into the balcony
at the sight of a paper kite,
at the passage of a dove's shadow;
then, a queue of roaches scatters at our coming.

in the fear of being frozen,
we melt the morning frost
in the heat of our mouth,
in between our rubbing palms.

night is a sea wave roaring us into hides,
yet sweeping waveson to the shore;
and like spoils of war, derelicts fill the
lacuna of their life with the vestige.

that is to say survival lifts us and shapes us
into heroes – we touch our fears and they release
smokes – incense that invite gods into our dwellings:
we propose to gods and they say 'yes.'

life as the bittersweet of coffee

i have understood fate in the irony of
detergent's wafting scent. to come
through the heat, you unmake your heart
a desert of grief into an orchard —where

chirping of crickets lull you at dusk &
flowerpeckers' wake you at dawn.
last night i stared at life & saw
a roadside chrysanthemum,

stuffed it in my mouth & my tongue
became a war-torn city,
my throat an aperture consuming a
continent with its roadblocks.

& when a stomach is protruded
with emptiness, it becomes a temple
no one dares enters barefooted
save a calvary of feasts, fit for the royalty.

but how do we enjoy crystals of the
day & escape darkness of the night?
but there are stars, moon, there are
meteors waiting to hatch our wishes.

demystification of grief, or, the augury of god is good all the time.

i put a butterfly on my tongue
a music serenading the night
into stars, turning darkness
into a harvest of melody.

i unfeathered a bird & a poem
fell off the sky: this is how a poet
leaves his chrysalis & perch
on a chrysanthemum.

this is how he brews himself
in advance for war, for peace,
for whatever will be
in the next ticks of time.

a boy asked for loan, granted,
looked at god from heart
rippling of gratitude; his god
wanted his desire come true.

a boy asked for loan, denied,
looked at god with eyes that
put down bridges. his god didn't
want him in the sea of debt.

how else do one stand ashore
waiting for the voice of god;
is the voice of man not
the voice of god?

wishbone by twilight

> *"when do we stop existing*
> *and start living?"*
> *—freezinpaul*

i wear life like a shirt with fifty gatos & tuck in silence

in the waist of my short. & in a love-painted house.

I became a cracked room, falling stone by stone.

a brittle fist holding the shorter part of a wishbone.

i run out of my body to unburden myself of myself.

& a maple leaf keeps my company in my new sanctuary.

last night, i plucked a lily. insurgency leaped out of its

pad. & ran into this dwelling with coloured cobwebs:

how does water live with fire? maybe i am a miracle.

a mud falling back into the mud bed at a bird's flight.

maybe i should follow the birds into the mouth of the moon.

maybe this planet is not for me, maybe it's just a playground.

this land wrongly picked me from an abacus & inked me

on this empty slate. last night, i touched my chest & felt

what it feels to clean my ear with a dove's feather.

i firm my grip on the wishbone. it feels like wormwood

yet my lips are shaped into the comeliness of laughter.

into what it feels when life is something to write home about

or write about home. these gifts i hold on my face are smiles

& silence. i cannot recall the number of wars my smiles

have won for me. the last i was regurgitating the list,

my tongue cried out of fatigue & slipped into a taciturn.

that's how i became an inferno surviving a waterfall.

silence is the wind blowing across the flowing fire.

that's how i give my mind a clean shave & declared

life as a warfield. & let god be the warrior, the sword.

the shield. and the war itself. while i only become

the twilight watching the scene of victory & vanquish.

the art of losing a name

i've feet-swept the earth
in search of wings for years
to later find it around my neck.

this is how life squeezes itself
into my throat & i become a stray
dolphin flailing at the seashore.

but it's time to float on the wind
& break its body the way a sword
travels the body of a plantain tree;

it's time to swim in the air,
to carry the sky on my back.
by this i mean i want to walk

into my dream & blow my trumpet
i want to whistle the way a
fledgeling walks out of the egg

& makes its first cry into the world's ears.
it's time for the bird in me to fly
this bird has been overfed with grief

it has been dragged in the mud
of agony with its face taking the
shape of an unswept kitchen.

i've got laughter erupt in my bowel,
while some erupt but die on arrival.
i've travelled to sokoto for wings
to later find it, pulsing in my sokoto;

saying the freedom we quest is not that far
it is the lines in the palms of our hands.

in my father's house;

they say geckos are kids of the landlord.
but father, a griot, never told us the tale
of being a reptile whose tail got lost;

it is a doorless home with no key. no lock.
secured by young slaves while away for war;

jànkárìwo are the ribbons fixed
to the ceiling-less roof, swinging back & forth;

they say it's a taboo to fall on man: fate of an
earthworm flailing in the jacuzzi of saltwater;

every splash is a bath. every ripple is a gulp.
every wave is a sickness. every whirl is fear.
every music is hope. every echo is a cadence
of the qur'an drooling from father's restless lips;

mother is a sea pushing dreams to the shore,
an amen to every prayer, a finger earthing curse,
god-filling every pothole of hunger and wishes;

Father's sweat is an air freshener welcoming all.
they say when you get old, you become a fragrance
that lasts and scents in the memory of your demise;

cats were legitimate friends. but today their shadows
are mere illusions that gives life to the dreams of rats

the house is a deserted temple. the children are guests.
some are strangers. some are waiting to return the day
the priest is declared no more. but my feet are doormats

into every room. my hands are portraits holding the pillars
by their wrists. for the monk is still hale and healthy.

father was a hoogle

father is the path to paradise
constructed beneath mother's feet.

he is the brightness in our smiles,
i lost count of the smiles he had drawn
on our faces, he's a proficient artist
prolific with his art of drawing smiles.

there is a window in his heart,
birds of tolerance fly in and
magnanimity threw out its hand
in the who-else-wants-to-come gesture.

father is a prophet: he preaches love:
that's obvious like the june-july rain,
and crystal like the september moon.

one day i told him the number of his
name, he has told the universe about it.
he is lavish with praise and encomium.
if i had taught him how to number names,

i'll see people of the underworld kneeling
at my feet washing it with gratitude.

father was hoopoe with heart of eagle:
call him a hoogle. today he is a parrot,
saying again what he had said a million times.

i see a lover still with the eagle heart
intoxicated with the wine of affection.
& i pray for him a blessed *shabe arus*
when he'll be married to his lover 'again.

alájobí

the eyes of the balcony was breathing fire,
so i entered the house through the backyard.
but i've become a masquerade,
if i wrongly enter a house or enter a
wrong house, who will dare expel me?

& if a masquerade has the
pele mark or the abaja mark,
no one knows, no one can tell;
save the awonimawoni who will
tell no one, who must never say.
and in the name of consanguinity,
i want to touch my heart; i want to
give it out. because, ordinarily, god
is the owner of my soul. he's the driver,
the bus and the fuel. but the dust on the
tail of my soul has held me down, and the
wind has been playing tric-trac on my spirit,
it should've come to blow the dust away;
god said i should pluck the leaf of pati-
ence because the wind coming is a
windstorm; it would've blown both
the dust, the feathers protecting
the tail and the bird of my soul.

but consanguinity is a spider
spinning its web to protect a house,
to detect men that have risen & fallen.
my hand warms my heart & i feel the
mildness of unwoven brocade & organza
fit for the peacock; my heart is not that

beautiful, but "sometimes, he makes clusters
of roses spring from the face of fire;
sometimes he throws bridges
across the face of the waters."

tonight, i don't want to be the fire,
i've got enough fire smithed me into existence.
into survival. i want to be the cluster of roses
pleasing the face of fires. i don't want to be the bridge
but i want to construct bridges so consanguine
(and a million others) will pass. we pass. yes!
we grow together. whereas, let whoever breaks
the bridges of consanguinity drown in rue
the scripture calls them *qaatilu rahim* and says
they will successfully make it to the bottom of hell.
& for good eggs, wa akhiru daawaana, alhamdulilahi.

how mother etches my name on god's palms

every night his face contests whiteness
        with the pages of his books.
as a calf he had mastered the craft
    of survival, him alone is a ten calvary –

an alfa – four hundred horses and
    six hundred foot. the last born:
            second of the twins, his tongue
the shape of my dreams. i want to

        open my eyes and see his dreams
perch, one by one, on the tree of reality.
and when i close my eyes, i'll know
    i've left for the world a fire, a moon,

a fighter, a winner. he hardly falls, and
    whenever he falls, i feed life to him,
        spoon by spoon. i call god to mount
    a garrison around him,

        that to where his head will become
a butterfly, the land a field of blossoms,
    his tongue a rainbow, may his legs take
the shape of marco polo and carry him.

[with mother on the way from ajilete]

[i said] [let mother's ears be] [closer to the ground than sands] [i would still fathom] [the language of the moment] [while standing] [so i climbed the hilltop] [to see the world] [but mother] [sitting on the temple mat] [described to me] [every fixtures & fittings] [of the landscape] [the ones i can and cannot see] [that day] [i saw home & away] [meeting at mother's tongue] [clearing their throats] [then rubbing their palms] [against mother's feet]

[eleven kilometers to arrive home] [i remember my stretched left palm] [a slate of stars] [i saw a star exploding into a comet] [even the bright of the day cannot veil its glee] [i imagined its tail made of cowries] [i imagined the bluntness of stones breathing sharpness into knives] [i imagined a rainbow raining its colours on us] [i imagined a gold mirror in my pouch] [seeing years to come] [& how to get there] [i heard a voice said so be it] [so be it] [in as few as i took from mother's breasts]

[seven kilometres to arrive home] [i remembered the war ahead] [how i alone must have to be ten calvary] [i held my head] [& it felt like i placed the city on it] [as if the world is leaning on my palm] [it felt like the mouth of a dagger slunk down my chest] [downtown my heart] [& like a town quieted by the aftermath of a tempest] [i heaved a deep sigh] [unto mother's backhand]

[three kilometers to arrive home] [i met my friends on the highway] [they said my outfit made me a gentleman] [the car's wiper swept away two wet leaves] [this is how life pulled me into consciousness] [into maturity] [into things that make strangers ask for my age] [even at mother's presence]

[one kilometer to arrive home] [i raise my head] [& my fear entered the sky's body] [i knew it got to the heaven] [it dropped a liquid that waxed my heart] [& my mind uncovered the dark space] [of meditation] [weapons of spiritual warfare] [fell in between mother's lips] [at home] [i picked my jalab] [rosary] [ablution kettle] [praying mat] [constructed an inner temple] [in mother's room]

64

ode to mother

i touch your feet and a paradise sprouts,

a meadow growing yes into the dreams of a gardener.

they call me a cat because i mew and curl at noises;

you say a community of rats crashes into fire at my yawn.

your tears are prayers. your smiles are ablutions.

every fire burning through your heath swims the night into light.

here, fire is not dangerous. we block the wind when making it,

and when it's made, we leave it at the mercy of wind.

i want to burn the weeds by your tabernacle

and become the moon of your temple.

you make a call to prayer. i want to make a hundred prostrations.

as a matter of wish blown into the hand of meteor,

i will make a thousand prostrations.

• • •

i touch myself where a tree was a node,
how [when dad arrived] we used to

fly into the street like pigeons,
like butterflies, like bees heading toward

a field of nectars. a boy's father arrived
& he became a rat, became a cockroach,

became a gecko fleeing to its hide.
the boy once told me he doesn't have a dad,

only a father. & his father said he doesn't
know how to spell his name. so

he decided to fill his heart with firestones.
but i read rumi where he said it is rain

that grows flowers, not thunder.
he did not know father spells

our names to us the way we sing
johnbull's name to him.

father did not call us fallen stars.
but meteor showers. a spark of wishes.

his tongue is wet with praise. like when
my siblings said my head was a burden

to my body, mother said this head
is a reservoir of knowledge, of wisdom.

voice and eyes as flagellation

before grandpa died, he used to say
when a parrot goes silent, check its throat,

fear must have built its nest therein,
its world must have been in danger. but

your silence is defined as a way a child begins
the act of stubbornness. so your mother says

"the husband of a stubborn child is cane."
but she forgets to add "eyes that carry

thorns & voice that strikes like thunder:"
every morning, father's voice breaks into

your body & stores dozens of thunderstones
in your ribcage. & at night, mother's eye cut

into your heart, so deep that your brain leaks
through it. your mind a pothole storing the

roadkill of the past. your present a bridge
leading to nowhere.

until you were reduced to talking to the only
person who understands your grief: yourself

before whom you can only talk confidently.
last night, you were counting & dictating the scars

their insurgencies left on your body to your confidant,
a voice of a comedian sounded from the

television. the joke dulled your pain, so much
that you laughed,

so hard that the room shifted its gaze to you
& you realized you were the only one

who heard the joke.
& the t.v. has been off.

boys are not stones

they no longer look at boys with flowery eyes

save ones that carry thorns on their stalks;

for boys to them are a community of rocks

impervious, a tapestry of muscles with concrete tendons,

until we're split into sinews sinewed into confused squadrons

and farmers begging to pluck laughter on the faces

of their own trees. we became a bevy of forgotten warriors

left to lose their ways from the red sea to the cold styx.

but boys are not stones, damn danger-prone.

we are once upon a time flowing stream stagnated

by bricks of abandonment, now carrying dirt and

dust on its sour-face. we became the wall clock

that has lost its hands, now making noisy ticks & ticks

like music sung with strange tongues.

boys are not stones but what you turned us into:

caskets of bones; even stones are seen

carrying [deep] scars of water on their bodies.

and girls are not cones, the deserving roses rained

on them [however] fell on them in a way

that says they are not only theirs.

i want to look myself in the mirror and see a god

but they say boys' skins /
            are harsher than the fleshes that melt into gods /
that god's hands are gentle tendons /
            handling bodies with care /
the way a scale weighs justice into the fate of man:

it clings its teeth to it / like a tick
sipping life from the skin of a bull;

it tilts to one side than the other /
and fractures its spine
            under the weight of one that is a bitter & salty lot /
while the other relieves it with treasure of smiles:

a girl assembles the stars on her teeth /
& a boy screams like a stream of dreams
falling over the body of a rock.

faith holds my hand & walks me into the future /
i want to hold its hand too /
                like a shell holding the body of a tortoise /
but what is fate if not a root knot /
no matter how early i arrive at the farm /
i find it welcoming.

but then /

i don't want to become an angel / only girls do/
i just want to become a salt in tasteless foods /
i want to become the yolk in forgotten eggs /
i want to look at myself in the mirror & see a god.

happenstance

i.
i licked harmattan off my lips,
a damsel passed by, my friends
said i licked off her clothes.
if man is to judge another,
we'd be busy slicing god into hell.
and nemesis they say is the only
child of god, it will be birthed and
will grow, catching up with man
with the flesh we've burnt.

ii.
when i flounder by,
they call me a balloon,
a sunup dew dissolving
into things by the seconds,
a lightweight champion.
but like muhammad ali,
i float like a butterfly and
sting like a bee. and when
the wind of this tempest
blow us off the balcony,
i swim on the back of the
air and swirl into bliss.
but the heavyweight lands
into shards, shrapnel.
and this paperweight lad
is no longer seen as a
weakling but a sundown
miracle wetting tongues
with serenades and sonnets.

li-fi

when innocence had its nest in boy's ribcage / he's hardly found where people sweep life out of cockroaches / even at sunset / you'll find the water of sunrise in his mouth / but society says to be patient is to become a patient of impecuniousness / you don't do with life in its pace / in your pace / you go in the pace of what's in vogue: to suck blood from others / with life's wi-fi: for that is what gives your life the glitter you seek // & gradually, woke-ness sinks morality into murky water / & preaches that instead of having the lion becomes the treasurer of the tiger / they'd rather do their hunt separately / so boy stepped over mannerism & brought down the cage of folly - to wear the inbox all day for feedback on his sent résumé / for to be complacent is to be a weakling / a trolley of vision without revision / a cup leaking antics and tactics / & to "wait" in his lexicon means "withering and imploding totally" / that waiting for your plant to become a tree / & the tree to bear flowers / & the flowers to beget fruits / is to die waiting for the crab's eyes to blink / that only the streetwise survives here: / it doesn't matter whether you carve your keyboard into a slate of oracle / to wring wealth out of the tears of others / it doesn't matter whether you send bullets to pluck people's breathe // & when nemesis sneaks behind boy's remote cauldron / & drags him behind the bar / the complacent kids become messiahs / & are beseeched to bend the backs of laws & statutes into a horse / so they may ride home the witty lad / alas / the only image the society paints of an impatient boy / is of a self-bitten finger / bitten so deep that it bleeds / a flood of blood.

to whom it may concern

the boy living in this body
is no longer interested, he is
giving up possession to fear,
to grief, to depression, or any other
thing that feeds on souls and turns
spirits into ashes, or any other thing
that is guilty of no crime yet prefers
prison, or any other thing that
when hit, wraps the leaf of
silence around its wrists.

there are many reasons why hitting
the bull on its eyes is no big deal:

1. his voice is already fire shaped
2. he walks a lion out of its den
3. the scars on people's body are his footprints
4. he's the weak wick that wears the temple dark
5. his body is a dark cloud rumbling for rain
6. he is a euphemism for insurgency, a ghoul
7. the pleasure of here is tiny compare to hereafter
8. this land on its own is a necropolis
9. too much gaps a century isn't enough to fill
10. full stop is better than a sentence, an execution

he is already nursing wounds
from a hit-and-run bull
as in there is a bomb ticking
in his body & he has no scars;
the wounds refuse to heal.

poem

this is how i title untitled poems
or how do we begin the sermon of a boy
tracing out sanity on the body of a dew-laden windscreen?

another time, he's found listening
to the music of dancing leaves.

maybe wellness is lurked
in the breeze that rushes through his body.

maybe he should chase wind
into the body of earth or sea.

maybe july will remind him that
dead plants will still rise as august visitors.

yes. the earth is a boa
it has swallowed things, & still counting;

but there are places
where it sprouts what it swallowed
by way of blossoms.

but a boy seeking peace in death
is a seed watered by depression,
& when iroko grows, it becomes an egoistic god
massaged with perpetual appeasements.

& the body of a boy carrying deep sighs
is a labyrinth of hot coals:
it burns things. even the title of a poem.

contours

the wrinkle-like contours on my face
are lines from the pain of love
pierced by the pieces of shattered heart.
i've been dribbled on the track of love
i'm not the dribbled. i'm the ball.
i've been playing. finding myself
under the pants of players.

love has made a hard guy, a paperweight champion.
so, where do we go from here – hotbed of lovers.
how do we see true love on foreheads.

love experience has made my heart
a hard disk backing up bitter experience:
the one i love doesn't love me,
the one who loves me is not truthful,
and others who love me, i cannot
find my bee making honey
from our intercourse.
and i'm not ready to sting one
who did not hit me.

but why is loving so cobwebby?
someone said it's because
we go crazy when we fall in love;
i laughed so wide: funny but true.
but why can't one who truly loves
meet one who truthfully loves him,
and then love her, unstintingly?

for i know true love truly exists.
yes, it's like a dove at it's sixth.

maybe i'll soon meet her.
maybe i've even found her.
but i've written many love poems in vain
so now, i start saving them in my veins

to an aborted future
for aishat morenikeji

i imagined the future & i saw myself
inserting a ring into your fingers & you

wrap yourself around me like a child
asking for a third packet of candies.

i saw myself on your campus while you
point out to your friends: ehh! my hubby,

a lawyer, poet. i wished to lead you
to the future with map of spirituality,

while we caress our infatuation into
affection and our affection into a love

seeing the light of god. i saw your feet
shaking on the line of two beliefs, but

your head & body are bent towards mine,
so i touched you the way a feather falls

on another, tilting you to my side
and pulling you into the inside of me.

i was away but my heart longed for home
to behold your spellbinding smile again.

i have said "okay" to your sudden "no"
but still carried the light of hope that,

one day, your lips will part ways & a
music of "yes" will fly out. sadly, the lips

didn't see the light of the day. it opened
one night & the liquor of death poured in.

hibiscus reminds me of her absence

for aishat morenikeji

i summon her sister to refresh my memory
of her flowery voice, how words leave her mouth
like hot beads escaping the cleavage of a machine.
keji's sister flashes her teeth and i see mirrors of her,
of how i measure her weight on my laps, in my arms,
and her length with my length as we stand staring into
each other's eyes as if to melt into one body.

tonight, i undress myself and a history of love war crashes
upon the mattress. i gather the ashes of her smiles
with the palms of my hand and keep them under my pillow.
the remnant of her is talcum powder,
i rub my face with it and become a script of gone diamond.

i still expect a miracle to bring her before me
raising two thumbs for remaining strong after her demise,
to take me to a farther land where she is living a fine life
counting the stars every night awaiting my arrival,
asking me to keep her existence a secret,
else she'll become a smoke of incense.

my tongue takes the shape of a dagger
sharpened with anger and cuts into the future,
my eyes make a nest of how life
would've carved two bodies into birds,
picking feeds into each other's mouths.

bird by bird, unfeathering my grief

i first knock the dove in me on the head
where a boy is a loyal camel carrying god as his hunch,
tracing love's footsteps, foot by foot;
today, i prefer this bird dead.

at the sight of a love hill;
sometimes i crawl into the shell of a snail,
sometimes i wear the body of a cheetah,
sometimes i am a peregrine falcon flying past its target,
sometimes i slip into the shell of a tortoise,
but all the times, i'm offered to a sudden fire to eat me
from sole to soul.

and when the pain of rue and
heartbreak meet in one's heart,
it sparks into a forest fire,
erasing the present and eating into the future.

my lover gave me a towel to mop my sweating palms,
i didn't know she's giving me something
i'll [later] use it to choke my leaking eyes.
my tears drop in a honey and it becomes a bile.
it drops in a milk and it clots into hope(lessness).
this morning, i threw the towel into the australian fire and
it went off.

if all my lovers were god, i'd finally believe
after elliott bradley

and last year
when our water eventually find
their ways to each other, we flowed
through a twin rock bending towards
god and became a two-stair waterfall.

i. you fed a rice into my mouth,
then a noodle that wouldn't digest
because my heart was busy panting

ii. you made two dishes for me
and insisted that i finished them
because the water that cooked
them was love, was bliss, was nuptial.

i. i touched your dimple and
it became a crescent. a glee
multiplying the sheen of your teeth.

ii. i poured a yoghurt for you, for me;
it didn't taste as usual. it tasted of
you, of the future we had drawn.

i. you call me a name that reminds
me of a caring sister that went
and never return

ii. you call me a name that means
the world and hereafter to me.

i. i said i love you,
you said you love me too

but the way god wants us
to love any random people,
for the sun of otherwise love
had set.

ii. i said i love you,
you said you love me too
provided i become a god
understanding every beat
of your heart because you are
not ready to interpret them.

i crush a flower into your throat
but they say fragrance is for the body.
should the inside of an angel
not hold water?

this is how i am daily reminded
of the one that went the elevator
while i was leading her up through
the staircase. she got to the top
but couldn't come out, come down.
beckoning. rubbing palms.

love is a flower in all ramifications.
this flower folds at a touch and
when left at the mercy of nature,
it spreads its arm touching north
and south. it's past midnight,
i put my rosary around my neck,
break a sachet of powder milk,
dip my finger into it and lick
the memory of you.
but here.

finding yourself

i.
you can't believe you've become a lone moon
seriously searching for a cloudless sky,
seriously searching your heart for a gemstone
you're tired of these fishing and hunting
how you stormed facebook last night
in search of jewels, as if facebook
is now a field where waterleaf is plucked:
& every flower is doing *kami kami kami.*

ii.
sometimes, you just want to escape
from yourself & run into the body
of a storm. you want to get tossed
like a coin, thrown like a dice &
see yourself landing on the right spot;
for the mat is spread on the right place,
the ladder is placed on the right place,
you want to be in a place where
you'll breath in yourself
from the body of an houri.

telephone call

you, now like a lonely lampshade,
shine an orange light in an empty room
asking life how you've become so.
how you now despise a voice you used to
leave everything in the world to attend to.

a voice that was already echoing in your
own lung oozing out through your oesophagus.
throat. tongue. lips.
this voice sounded to you like the
voice of the world when it falls from the
telephone's mouth into your left ear,
& you felt the music & tonality shouldn't stop.

a voice you regarded as voice of voices

the voice is now the peel of melon seed:
a taboo that shouldn't be seen in the morn,
now you got your face phone-lit
by incoming calls from the voice
but you never activated the green button
for the voice to come to life again,
for this voice was cut (caught) red-handed
and the world became a flood of blood.

and now, you wade through the water of
memory like a toad escaping a fisherman's
hook, and you realized that in life (today's
world) not all holidays are holy days.

you had thought this voice will be a music
to welcome you when you've gone out

at daybreak into the fog to pluck figs
for your romantic weekend's breakfasts.

you sighed a sealed breath like a signed
deed then you remember it's been a while
that you hear from your father –
a voice at its eld yet never grow old,
filled with litanies soaked in rhymes and
rhythms that carry brightness into the
sunshine as he wagged his old tongue in prayers

a voice that has never betrayed you.

you remember the last time you spoke
sitting on his bedside, how his joyful glance
pierced your skin until your body
became a clay carrying carved letters,
letters that blaze so deep that they
became messages of fire across the sky.

you carried these thought out of your
breastbone into the very back of your mind,
except that your father's voice kept echoing
in voluptuous astonishment in your head
and you told your new friend the tales of
sixty meteors that fell in past hour:
"oh friend! let's go pay homage to the night
and in the morrow meet at sunup."

the speared & the spared

you wonder how life pushes you
from peripheral to the center
in fact, you become the centre
the power place. the breastbone
of influence. the cornerstone
of authority. the gemstone
you remember those who were
speared through your journey up
you remember those drowned
in the dark ocean of survival
you remember those blown away
by windstorm after a heartbreak,
you remember how the mighty fell
and you dissolve into prostration
to the lord who got you spared

stroke of serendipity

from the sea of my body,
my dreams chased my fear ashore
its wave wet my feet and burnt
the earthworm of my hope.

i picked artefacts in the hoofprints
of horses: one the shape of "y",
the other the shape of "s,"
i walk the beach for hours
in search of "e;"

i didn't know i've been
painting the shore
with the "yes" of my footprints.

a lantern flickers from the extreme,
its weak wick dimming out
like an intermission
between life and death.

i scratched the surface of my
suntanned memories with a
falcon's talon, it bled possibility;
a horse ran out of the wound
and began circumambulating me,

neighing:
that every road we took in the past
still leads to the colourful future.

it came with a gun and tied around its
handle was a kerchief of house-dust:

mother said when one receives
a gun with house-dust,
the universe just wrote
you a solidarity letter;

i smiled and entered the sea
of my body, looking back,
i felt like following [again] the
outgoing tide as it crashed
upon itself,
upon the shore.

someday i will be no more
after rasak malik gbolahan

this house will become a memory of me, a museum of my existence holding
the regalia i've worn on its walls, hanging my frames and poems, holding
unto my rosaries as if to leave them is to shift its foundation. someday
my heart will stop beating but my wristwatch will keep ticking; and i will
be ushered out of this house and lowered into dust. sometime at night,
people will enter the house and ask if there's anybody left outside, someone
will say "no" and they will shut the door leaving me outside in the grave.
someday people will call for a praying mat to pray and they will be given
my mat, they will remember me and recite ikhlas upon my soul. someone
will sit at my corner to mimic how i smile while drawing close the beads
of my rosary or while meditating or rubbing my cats on their heads or
writing my poems or thinking of the day i will be no more. someday i will
be no more and the only thing that will remain of me is the memory of me.

acknowledgements

my thanks to the editors of the following journals and anthologies where some of the verses in this book have previously appeared: *agbowo,lucent dreaming, the pangolin review, vortices of verses, today i choose joy, splendor of dawn, fireflies light, the banyan review, the quills, the giant pen, the speaking heart, boys are not stones anthology, a country of broken boys anthology, and Ebedi Review.*

About the Author

Taofeek Ayeyemi, fondly called Aswagaawy, is a Nigerian lawyer, writer, and author of the chapbook *Tongueless Secrets* (Ethel Press, 2021) and a collection *aubade at night or serenade in the morning* (Flowersong Press, 2021). His works have appeared or forthcoming in *CV2, Lucent Dreaming, Ethel-zine, Up-the-Staircase Quarterly, ARTmosterrific, Banyan Review, Presence, tinywords, the QuillS,* and elsewhere. He won the 2021 Loft Books Flash Fiction Contest, 2018 Poetic Wednesday Poetry Contest, Honorable Mention Prizes in 2020 Stephen A. DiBiase Poetry Prize, 2020 Akita International Haiku Contest, 2020 Fujisan Taisho International Tanka Contest, and 2nd Prize in 2016 Christopher Okigbo Poetry Prize. He is @ Aswagaawy on Facebook and Twitter. When he's not in the court arguing, in the chambers drafting, in the bedchamber with his cats poeticizing or meditating as a Sufi, he'll be somewhere in the world talking.

www.ingramcontent.com/pod-product-compliance
Lightning Source LLC
Chambersburg PA
CBHW030646190726
48286CB00008B/2683